More brilliant SAT Busters for KS2 Maths and English...

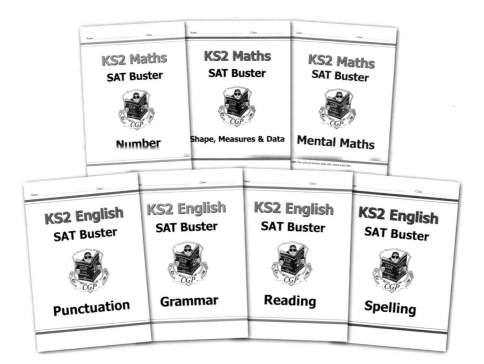

KS2 Maths SAT Buster — Number

KS2 Maths SAT Buster — Shape, Measures & Data

KS2 Maths SAT Buster — Mental Maths

KS2 English SAT Buster — Punctuation

KS2 English SAT Buster — Grammar

KS2 English SAT Buster — Reading

KS2 English SAT Buster — Spelling

...have you got yours?

See them all at www.cgpbooks.co.uk
— or ask your teacher for more info!

ISBN 978 1 84146 175 5

9 781841 461755

E6P22   £3.95
                (Retail Price)

www.cgpbooks.co.uk

KR-920-878

It's another Quality Book from CGP

This book has been carefully written for Key Stage Two children learning punctuation. It's full of tricky punctuation exercises designed to give lots of practice for the Year 6 SATs.

Children can use the Punctuation Python tick boxes for self-assessment, which helps you work out how they're getting on.

What CGP is all about

Our sole aim here at CGP is to produce the highest quality books — carefully written, immaculately presented and dangerously close to being funny.

Then we work our socks off to get them out to you — at the cheapest possible prices.

Punctuation Hints and Tips

Some punctuation can be a bit tricky. If you get stuck, this page might help you out.

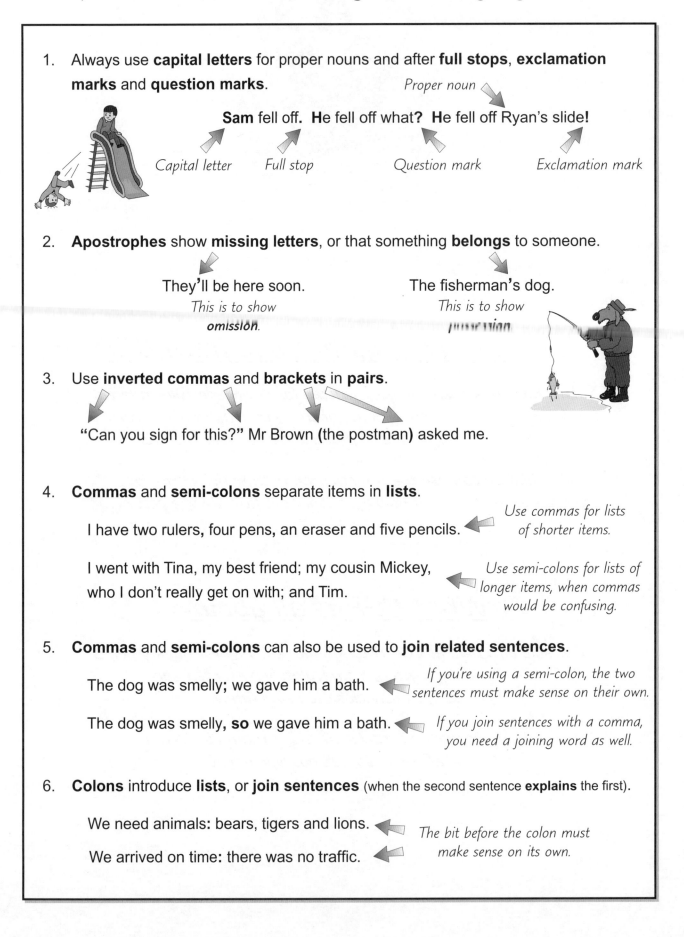

1. Always use **capital letters** for proper nouns and after **full stops**, **exclamation marks** and **question marks**.

   Proper noun

   Sam fell off. **H**e fell off what? **H**e fell off Ryan's slide!

   Capital letter   *Full stop*   *Question mark*   *Exclamation mark*

2. **Apostrophes** show **missing letters**, or that something **belongs** to someone.

   They'll be here soon.
   This is to show omission.

   The fisherman's dog.
   This is to show possession.

3. Use **inverted commas** and **brackets** in **pairs**.

   "Can you sign for this?" Mr Brown (the postman) asked me.

4. **Commas** and **semi-colons** separate items in **lists**.

   I have two rulers, four pens, an eraser and five pencils.
   Use commas for lists of shorter items.

   I went with Tina, my best friend; my cousin Mickey, who I don't really get on with; and Tim.
   Use semi-colons for lists of longer items, when commas would be confusing.

5. **Commas** and **semi-colons** can also be used to **join related sentences**.

   The dog was smelly; we gave him a bath.
   If you're using a semi-colon, the two sentences must make sense on their own.

   The dog was smelly, **so** we gave him a bath.
   If you join sentences with a comma, you need a joining word as well.

6. **Colons** introduce **lists**, or **join sentences** (when the second sentence **explains** the first).

   We need animals: bears, tigers and lions.
   We arrived on time: there was no traffic.
   The bit before the colon must make sense on its own.

Contents

Published by CGP

Contributors

David Broadbent, Heather Gregson, Luke von Kotze, Anthony Muller, Jennifer Underwood

With thanks to Claire Boulter and Maxine Petrie for the proofreading.

ISBN: 978 1 84146 175 5

www.cgpbooks.co.uk

Clipart from CorelDRAW®

Printed by Elanders Ltd, Newcastle upon Tyne.

Based on the classic CGP style created by Richard Parsons.

Section 1 — Basic Punctuation

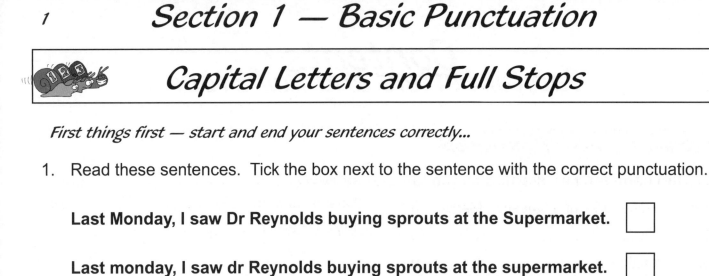

Capital Letters and Full Stops

First things first — start and end your sentences correctly...

1. Read these sentences. Tick the box next to the sentence with the correct punctuation.

    Last Monday, I saw Dr Reynolds buying sprouts at the Supermarket. ☐

    Last monday, I saw dr Reynolds buying sprouts at the supermarket. ☐

    Last Monday, I saw Dr Reynolds buying sprouts at the supermarket. ☐

2. Circle the words in the box which should always start with a capital letter.

    spectacular   dishwasher   cairo

    italy

    wednesday   armchair
                          concrete

                    neighbour   pineapple
    unlucky   mr jacob

    august   sarah   town

3. Rewrite these sentences, adding in capital letters where they are needed.

    there are roadworks on oaktree road.

    ....

    mrs parker gave oliver extra homework.

    ....

    my uncle supports leeds united.

    ....

Capital Letters and Full Stops

4. Rewrite these sentences with capital letters and full stops in the correct places.

   the hamster was startled by the loud noise

   ....

   nobody expected the cake to taste of cabbage

   ....

5. The words in this sentence are all jumbled up. Rewrite the sentence in the correct order and add capital letters and a full stop where they are needed.

to	groooc	thursday	is	golng	sandra	on

   ....

6. There are **six** mistakes in the use of capital letters and full stops in this paragraph. Rewrite the paragraph and correct the mistakes.

   > penguins are a type of bird that cannot fly Most penguins spend half their time hunting for food in the water. penguins are well adapted to life in the ocean they can move and see better under water than on land

   ....

   ....

   ....

   ....

   ....

Punctuation Pythons get capital letters and full stops right in their sleep. Can you? Put a tick in the appropriate box.

Exclamation Marks and Question Marks

There's no getting round it — you need to know all about these punctuation gems...

1. Draw lines to match these sentences to the correct punctuation mark.

   Where is the time machine   .

   Get out of my room   ?

   The day was warm and sunny   !

   Use exclamation marks to show strong emotion or to emphasise a point.

2. Draw a line to match each of these sentences to the correct punctuation mark.

   ?

   What time is it

   Look out

   That's amazing   **Go away**

   Should we leave

   I'm asking you to sit down

   I'm so happy   **Who did this**

   !

3. These sentences have been mixed up.
   Write them out correctly and add the correct punctuation.

   are   door   you   the   hiding   why   behind

   ....

   appeared   my   in   dinosaurs   two   cupboard

   ....

   carry   can   help   this   you   me   piano

   ....

Exclamation Marks and Question Marks

4. Draw a line to match the two parts of these exclamations so that they make sense.

I'm so pleased   glass vase!

Watch out for   that you've come!

Don't drop the   day ever!

It was the best   falling rocks!

5. Complete each of these sentences with an exclamation mark or a question mark.

a. My pet spider has escaped.....

b. I don't want to go.....

c. Can you open this.....

d. Stop making so much noise.....

e. Are you going into space.....

f. Have you seen this film before.....

g. My brother is a monster.....

h. Do you know William.....

i. Has anyone found my hat.....

j. That's disgusting.....

6. For each of these word pairs, write down a question which includes both words.

elephant   **trunk**

....

shoes   **purple**

....

neighbour   **alien**

....

Do you know how to use question marks?
Punctuation Pythons do! Tick a box to show how you've done.

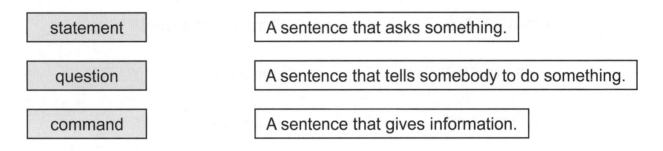

Sentences

Get your noggin around the difference between statements, questions and commands...

1. Draw lines to match these sentence types to the correct definition.

    | statement | | A sentence that asks something. |

    | question | | A sentence that tells somebody to do something. |

    | command | | A sentence that gives information. |

2. Read these sentences and write down whether each one is a question or a statement.

    What do you think of my coat?   ....

    There's no food in the cupboard.   ....

    Did he arrive in time for his interview?   ....

    We are going to leave soon.   ....

    Did the flying saucer land on Sarah's roof?   ....

3. Read these sentences. Tick the box next to all of the commands.

    a. I've asked you to clean your room fifty times.

    b. Shut the window before you leave the house!

    c. You never listen to what your hamster says.

    d. I wish you'd come to the theme park on Saturday.

    e. Don't start playing tiddlywinks now!

    f. Finish your dinner, including the Brussels sprouts!

Sentences

4. Read these pairs of sentences. Circle the version with the most suitable punctuation.

There were fish in the bed!	There were fish in the bed.
I left the room.	I left the room!
They stopped for a rest!	They stopped for a rest.
The aliens have found me.	The aliens have found me!
I turned around!	I turned around.

5. Write out these sentences with either a full stop or a question mark at the end.

What time does the play start

....

Should we hide the chocolates in the safe

....

Mrs Robinson asked if my homework was complete

....

6. Put an 'S' in each box after a statement, and a 'C' in each box after a command.

a. Stay away from me. ☐

b. I go to school every day. ☐

c. Keep out of here. ☐

d. Don't do that again. ☐

e. I've forgotten my own name. ☐

f. Don't feed the ducks. ☐

g. Pigs are my favourite pets. ☐

h. Walk on the pavement. ☐

Sentences

7. Draw a line to show whether each sentence is a statement, question or command.

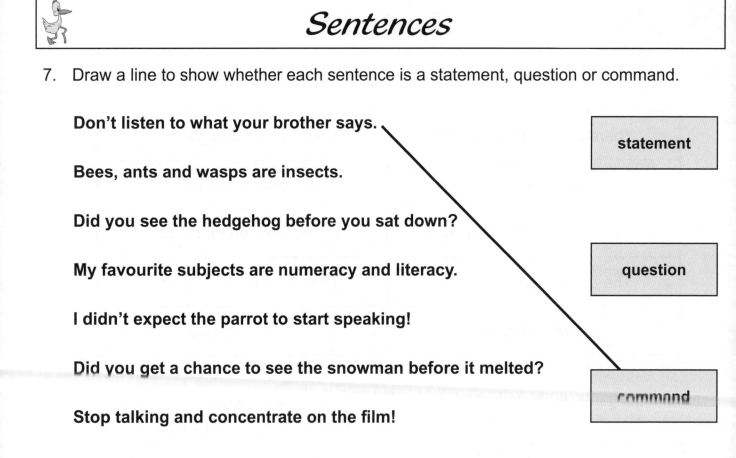

Don't listen to what your brother says.

Bees, ants and wasps are insects.

Did you see the hedgehog before you sat down?

My favourite subjects are numeracy and literacy.

I didn't expect the parrot to start speaking!

Did you get a chance to see the snowman before it melted?

Stop talking and concentrate on the film!

statement

question

command

8. Look at this sentence.

Go away and leave me alone!

Why has an exclamation mark been used?

....

....

9. Write a question, a statement and a command.

Question: ....

Statement: ....

Command: ....

Sentences

10. Here are some statements. For each, write down what the question could be.

    a.   ....

         Answer: I enjoy swimming, playing football and playing the guitar.

    b.   ....

         Answer: We went camping in France and went swimming in the sea.

    c.   ....

         Answer: I have two brothers and a younger sister.

11. Rewrite these statements as questions. Use the correct punctuation.

You can speak French.	Can you speak French?
They broke the plate.	....
The cat fell into the river.	....
I am feeling tired.	....

12. Write whether each of these sentences is a **statement**, **question** or **command**.

Speak louder	....
I can't whistle	....
Does this work	....

Mixed Practice

Here are some questions to test everything you've learnt in this section so far...

1. Read this sentence.

    > **Everyone knew that Julia was the fastest runner in the class.**

    Why does **Julia** start with a capital letter?

    ....

    ....

2. Draw a line to match each sentence to the correct punctuation mark.

    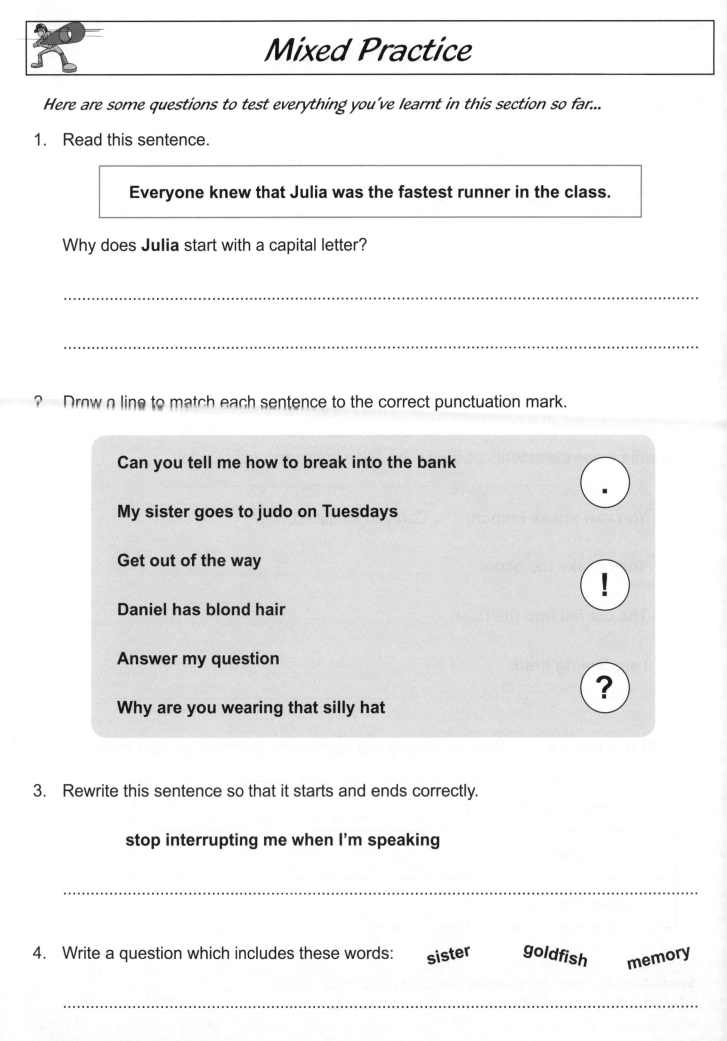

    Can you tell me how to break into the bank

    My sister goes to judo on Tuesdays   .

    Get out of the way

    Daniel has blond hair   !

    Answer my question

    Why are you wearing that silly hat   ?

3. Rewrite this sentence so that it starts and ends correctly.

    stop interrupting me when I'm speaking

    ....

4. Write a question which includes these words: sister   goldfish   memory

    ....

Mixed Practice

5. Write whether each of these sentences is a **question**, **statement** or **command**.

    Sahid found a fly in his cup of tea   ....

    Stop writing and put your pens down   ....

    I can't believe you don't like chocolate   ....

    Can you turn off the radio   ....

    We need a plumber to fix the bath   ....

6. Draw a line to match each sentence to the correct punctuation mark.

    Stand in a straight line | ? |

    Our hamster is called Bill | . |

    When shall we leave | ! |

7. Rewrite this passage with the correct punctuation (hint: there are **five** mistakes).

    > When you're in rome, you should visit the Colosseum. it is a huge
    > structure and it could hold up to 50 000 people? Can you imagine
    > what it would be like to be a gladiator in such a Spectacular building.

    ....

    ....

    ....

    ....

You've finished the section! How did you do?
Tick the box that shows what kind of Python you are.

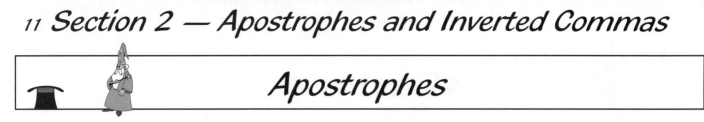

Apostrophes

Apostrophes can show that a letter, or some letters, are missing.

1. Draw a line between each set of words and the correct **contraction** (short version). Watch out, some of them are wrong and don't have a matching pair.

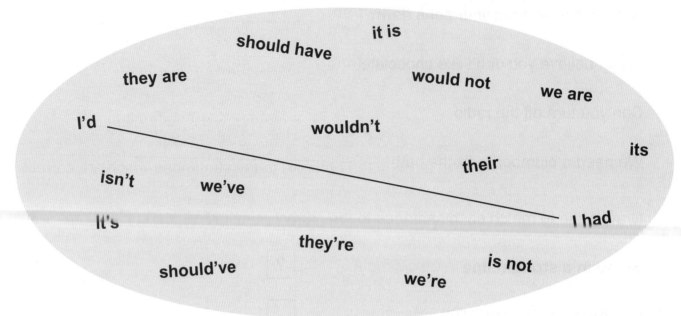

2. Underline the correct word in bold in each sentence.

    I think we **couldv'e / could've** got to the cinema at the right time.

    Joseph wished his mother **hadn't / had'nt** made pickle and jam sandwiches.

    My horse **won't / wo'nt** jump over any fences unless she's had a sugar lump.

3. Rewrite the words below as a **contraction**.

    I am   ....   Cannot   ....

    You are   ....   Might have   ....

    Did not   ....   Will not   ....

Apostrophes

4. Look at the sentences below. The correct sentence is ....

   A **This is Freds meteor rock collection.**

   B **This is Freds' meteor rock collection.**

   Apostrophes also show if something belongs to someone.

   C **This is Fred's meteor rock collection.**

5. Read these sentences. Put a tick in the box next to the sentences which are correct.

   a. My car's engine will not start. ☐

   b. My fishs' tank needs to be cleaned. ☐

   c. Chloes' book had fallen into a puddle. ☐

   d. They say he's New York's best detective. ☐

   e. The childs's swing needs repairing. ☐

   f. Don't go in there, that's the monster's room. ☐

6. For each pair of words, write a sentence using **apostrophes** and the given words.

   guitar   hamster

   ....

   dinosaur   sister

   ....

Section 2 — Apostrophes and Inverted Commas

Apostrophes

7. Draw lines to match the sentences which mean the same thing.

The dress that belongs to a girl		The girls' dresses
The dress that belongs to two girls		The girl's dress
Two dresses that belong to two girls		The girls' dress

8. These sentences are written incorrectly. Rewrite them so that they are correct.

My aunts house is haunted by a smelly ghost.

....

The childrens presentation was very interesting.

....

Both of my daughters husbands are terrible cooks.

....

9. Rewrite each sentence so that it changes from **singular** to **plural**. ⬅ *'Singular' means one. 'Plural' means more than one.*

Singular	Plural
That's my cousin's magic carpet.	That's my cousins' magic carpet.
The tree's leaves are yellow.	
It's dark in the witch's hut.	
The child's toys were new.	

Apostrophes

10. Write the correct word to finish each sentence.

   their/they're: I really hope .... coming to the party.

   your/you're: I think it is .... turn next.

   were/we're: .... going on holiday next week.

11. Complete these sentences with **its** or **it's**. ⬅

   Don't forget:
   It's means 'it is'.
   Its means belongs to 'it'.

   I'm so happy that .... snowing.

   Did you know that .... eyes are as big as dinner plates?

   .... home is in the rings around Saturn.

   I think .... a shame that you're not going to play rugby.

12. Underline the correct word for each sentence.

   Hey, **they're / their** cheating!

   Were / We're leaving before the yak gets back.

   Your / You're dinner is getting cold.

   What **were / we're** you thinking?

   This is **they're / their** new pet elephant.

   I don't think **your / you're** helping.

Punctuation Pythons are ace with apostrophes.
Tick the box that shows how ace you are.

Section 2 — Apostrophes and Inverted Commas

Inverted Commas

Time to get cracking on some inverted commas (speech marks).

1. Tick the sentence which is correct.

    "Step away from the cabbage!" he shouted. ☐

    "Step away from the cabbage"! he shouted. ☐

    "Step away from the cabbage! he shouted." ☐

2. Tick which sentences have inverted commas in the correct place.
    Fix the sentences which are wrong by adding inverted commas.

    a. "Look out!" she shouted, "There's a giant mole!" ☐

    b. "You'll call me?" Mum asked, After five o'clock? ☐

    c. "I hope that goblin knows the way, she sighed. ☐

    d. Sally grumbled, "I'll take Scamp for a walk later." ☐

3. This paragraph is missing some inverted commas. Fix the paragraph by putting
    inverted commas in the correct boxes.

    **Jeanne was disappointed with her performance today. ☐ She explained,
    ☐ I just don't think I was able to shoot as well as I expected,"
    before ☐ adding, ☐ I'll have to try ☐ harder ☐ next time. ☐**

4. Read these pairs of sentences. Circle the sentences that contain **direct speech**.

"Don't leave me at home!"	I told her not to leave me at home.
"I won't sulk," she grumbled.	She grumbled that she wouldn't sulk.
She said the troll was not invited.	"The troll is not invited," she said.

Inverted Commas

5. Rewrite these sentences using **direct speech**.

   I said that the house was painted tartan.

   ....

   I asked Raj to wait for me in the car park.

   ....

   He told me that he wants to be an astronaut.

   ....

6. Use the words in the box to write a sentence using **direct speech**.

snails	wizard	roared	spell

   ....

   ....

7. Rewrite the paragraph below, using **direct speech**.

   **The fireman told me that this was the biggest fire he had ever
   had to deal with. He said he had been fighting fires for
   15 years, but he could not remember one that was so fierce.**

   ....

   ....

   ....

   ....

Inverted Commas

8. Draw lines to match these sentences to the correct term.

    "I've got maths on Monday morning."

    He told me that he really likes snail soup.

    She said she was going to Paris in March.

    "I want to ride on the steam engine!"

    reported speech

    direct speech

9. Rewrite this sentence using **reported speech**.

    "A monkey has stolen my glasses!" Nico shouted.

    ....

10. Use the words in the box to write a sentence using **reported speech**.

seen	Sunil	asked	kangaroo

    ....

    ....

11. Read this sentence.

    Juan told me about the time when he lived in Barcelona.

    How do you know that this sentence is **reported speech**?

    ....

    ....

Inverted Commas

12. Read the conversation below. Write down what Karim said in **reported speech**.

"I've never been to ancient Egypt," complained Karim, "Can you take me?"

"Time travel is dangerous," replied his mother, "I can't take you everywhere."

"I'll behave," he promised, "I was good with the dinosaurs, wasn't I?"

....

....

....

....

13. Rewrite the conversation below in **reported speech**.

Claire: "Sachin, did you enjoy your holiday in Africa?"

Sachin: "I did, and I saw a lion."

Claire: "Were you scared?"

Sachin: "No, the lion was friendly and I gave him a sandwich."

....

....

....

....

....

....

Punctuation Pythons love hissstory... and using inverted commas correctly. Tick the box if you're a python too.

Section 2 — Apostrophes and Inverted Commas

Mixed Practice

These pages have some questions on apostrophes and inverted commas all jumbled together.

1. The sentence below has **apostrophes** and **inverted commas** in the wrong place.
    Rewrite the sentence with the correct punctuation.

    'Great! It"s beans and jelly for dinner tonight," Wayne thought,
    "and that"s my favourite meal!'

    ....

    ....

2. Write a sentence using **direct speech** which includes these words: you're   your

    ....

3. Draw a line to match the two parts of these **contractions** so that they make sense.

    I   't

    could   'm

    won   n't

4. Write the full version of each underlined **contraction** in the box provided.

    "Well, you <u>could've</u> reminded me you were going. I <u>didn't</u> remember."

    "Don't worry, <u>I'll</u> give it back as soon as I can. You <u>won't</u> notice it's missing."

Mixed Practice

5. Fill in the gaps in the table.

Reported Speech	Direct Speech
He said he was going to the park.	"I'm going to the park," he said.
He said he needed time to think.	
	"I'll arrive soon," I said.
She told me that she liked geese.	

6. Rewrite this sentence with the correct punctuation.

   When are we going to get there? he asked, Im tired!

   ....

7. There are five punctuation mistakes in this paragraph.
   Rewrite the paragraph and correct the mistakes.

   Hannahs' mum stayed up all night preparing her daughters's surprise
   party. She'd made a beautiful cake: it's icing was pink and blue.
   "Hannah, she called up the stairs, could you come to the kitchen, please?"

   ....

   ....

   ....

   ....

   ....

Snakes alive! That was a tricky section. How do you think
you got on? Tick one of the boxes to show how you did.

Commas

To write well, you have to get to grips with commas...

1. Each of these sentences is missing a comma. Put a comma
   in one of the boxes to make each sentence correct.

   I couldn't ☐ find my hat ☐ my gloves or ☐ my satchel.

   I would like a ☐ pen pal ☐ from Mexico ☐ Spain or Colombia.

   My sister ☐ took me ☐ to the ice rink ☐ the cinema and the ☐ restaurant.

2. Rewrite these sentences, adding in commas where they are needed.

   Andy Mark and Caroline took their dog for a walk.

   ....

   We bought carrots and a cabbage for our donkey.

   ....

   Anja plays tennis squash darts and table tennis.

   ....

3. Use the words in the box to complete the sentence below.
   Remember to add commas in the right places.

a pencil	**a piece of string**	**a compass**

   I always carry ....

   and a pound coin in case of emergencies.

Commas

4. Tick the box next to the sentence with the comma in the correct place.

    Although, they were very hungry they wouldn't eat the sausages.   ☐

    Although they were very hungry, they wouldn't eat the sausages.   ☐

    Although they were very hungry they wouldn't eat, the sausages.   ☐

5. Rewrite each sentence, adding the words in the box in the right place, using commas. The first one has been done for you.

    Raisins are my favourite snack.   **which are dried grapes**

    Raisins, which are dried grapes, are my favourite snack.

    Tracy told me I should go.   **who is my best friend**

    ....

    My house is near the canal.   **which has a blue door**

    ....

6. The box below contains a sentence that's been jumbled up. Draw a line from the beginning of the sentence to the end, going through the punctuation marks in the right places.

    who is 84 years old

    ,

    .

    ,

    she couldn't find my tortoise

    Despite trying really hard

Commas

7. Some of these sentences are missing commas. Add the commas into the sentences.
    Some of the sentences are correct already.

© CGP 2012

I had steak and chips for my dinner.

After snooker pool is my favourite game.

Carmen plays the banjo the piano and the guitar.

I locked my bicycle which is blue and green by the factory.

The town hall's brass bell rings four times every hour.

8. Use the phrases in the box to make a complete sentence.
    Remember to add commas where they are needed.

> won the lottery yesterday
>
> Martin's dad
>
> who has always been lucky

....

....

....

9. Rewrite these sentences, adding in commas where they are needed.

Sean Saeed Mike and Paula chased the llamas.

....

Although they're beautiful sharks are fast and deadly.

....

Unless they're yours the books pencils and pens stay here.

....

....

© CGP 2012

Commas

10. This paragraph is missing some commas. Fix the paragraph by putting commas in the correct boxes.

Although I enjoy it ☐ being a farmer ☐ isn't easy. You have to be ☐

fit ☐ healthy and strong. Even when the weather is bad ☐ the best

thing about the job ☐ is being ☐ outdoors. Every day I look after ☐

my sheep ☐ pigs ☐ chickens and geese.

11. This sentence is missing some words. Add words of your own so that the sentence makes sense and is punctuated correctly.

This cat, ... ,

has ears which are .... , ... and ....

12. There are **three** commas missing in this paragraph. Rewrite the paragraph, adding in the commas.

> **Although it takes a while you have to learn how the different pieces move. Monsters trolls and sorcerers can all move right across the board in one go but the giant can only move one square at a time.**

....

....

....

....

....

Punctuation Pythons always put their commas in the right places. Tick one of the boxes to show how you got on.

Hyphens

Hyphens join together two words, or two parts of a word...

1. Circle the version of 'a man eating tiger' that best fits the description in bold.

    a-man-eating-tiger   a man eating tiger

    A tiger that eats people

    a man-eating tiger   a man-eating-tiger

2. Underline the word from the last two columns that best fits the description in the first column. The first one has been done for you.

mark something again	remark	<u>re-mark</u>
go back to something	return	re-turn
say no to something	refuse	re-fuse
cover something again	recover	re-cover
remember something	recall	re-call

3. Each sentence is missing one hyphen. Put the hyphen in the correct box.

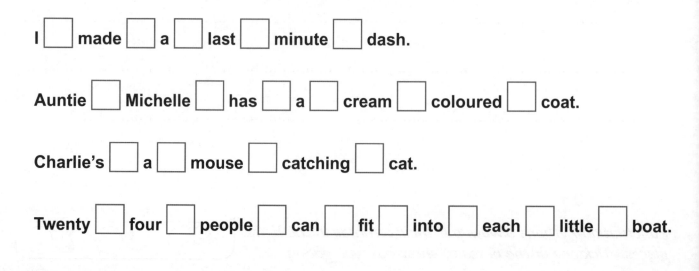

I ☐ made ☐ a ☐ last ☐ minute ☐ dash.

Auntie ☐ Michelle ☐ has ☐ a ☐ cream ☐ coloured ☐ coat.

Charlie's ☐ a ☐ mouse ☐ catching ☐ cat.

Twenty ☐ four ☐ people ☐ can ☐ fit ☐ into ☐ each ☐ little ☐ boat.

Hyphens

4. Use each of these words in a sentence.

    first-class   ....

    middle-aged   ....

    half-eaten   ....

    custard-stained   ....

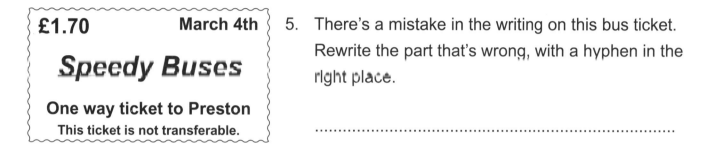

£1.70   **March 4th**

Speedy Buses

One way ticket to Preston
This ticket is not transferable.

5. There's a mistake in the writing on this bus ticket. Rewrite the part that's wrong, with a hyphen in the right place.

    ....

6. There are **four** hyphens missing in this paragraph. Rewrite the paragraph, adding in the hyphens.

    Twenty one people helped to fix my great grandmother's shed.
    They had a great time doing it. I helped out by recovering the roof with felt.
    Afterwards, we all had some old fashioned lemonade.

    ....

    ....

    ....

    ....

    ....

There's nothing a Punctuation Python likes more than a well-placed hyphen. Tick a box to show how you've done.

Brackets

Brackets (like this) go around any extra bits of information in a sentence...

1. Each of these sentences is missing a pair of brackets. Write them in.

    Mozart 1756-1791 is my favourite composer .

    My dad's car a Morris Minor is very noisy .

    There's more information about catching vampires later in the book see page 21 .

    We cycled through three counties Kent, Surrey and Sussex in three days .

2. Here are some sentences about brackets. Put a circle around the ones that are true.

    > **If you take all of the words in the brackets away, it should still leave a proper sentence.**
    >
    > **Brackets always come in pairs.**
    >
    > **You can't have any other punctuation between a pair of brackets.**
    >
    > **Brackets do the same job as a full stop.**

3. Each of these sentences only has one bracket. Put the other one in the correct box.

    I always buy ☐ a ☐ newspaper ☐ The Gazette) and a book of stamps.

    The dog (a spaniel ☐ had memorised ☐ his ☐ speech about biscuits.

    "There's a book ☐ on climbing (I think it's by Erica Smyth ☐ by the ☐ door."

    There are ☐ thirteen routes (three of them ☐ difficult ☐ through the woods.

© CGP 2012

Brackets

4. Rewrite these sentences so that the brackets are used correctly.

    Mark tells lots of stories (some of them are true! .

    ....

    My birthday (the 1st June is always sunny) .

    ....

    The winning ticket (number 452(belonged to an alien .

    ....

5. There are three pairs of missing brackets in this paragraph from a postcard.
    Add the missing brackets so that the paragraph makes sense.

    **After we left you, the journey took ages the flight was delayed , so we got in
    very late. Straight after breakfast cold meat and rolls we headed down to the
    beach. After going sunbathing it was thirty-two degrees! , we found a little
    coffee shop and had some cake.**

6. Write something in the gaps between the brackets to complete these sentences.

    It was in the summer of 1846 (..) that I
    first learnt to talk to the animals.

    The last day of term (...) can't come too soon.

    Mrs Mox (...) is sleeping in the corner.

---

*Punctuation Pythons always have a spare pair of
brackets in their pockets. Have you? Give yourself a tick.*

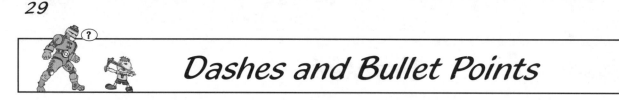

Dashes and Bullet Points

Using dashes will show your reader that you've got real style.

1. Write out each of these sentences correctly, using a pair of dashes for each one.

   Losing your shoes even old shoes is foolish.

   ....

   Tia I can't stress this enough was the real winner.

   ....

   Those cats the ones over there smell of mint.

   ....

2. The box below contains a sentence that's been jumbled up. Draw a line from the beginning of the sentence to the end, going through the punctuation marks in the right places.

   Lucky old Jermaine

   —

   got to take me to bowling   ▪   **the Jermaine who works at the chip shop**

   —

3. Write something in the gap between the dashes to complete the sentence.

   You can never tell what Henry — ....

   .... — will get up to next.

Dashes and Bullet Points

4. The dashes in these sentences are in the wrong place. Copy each sentence out with
    the dash in the right place.

    I'm not sure who did it it was — someone in this classroom.

    ....

    We had done all we could it was time to go home —.

    ....

    — They had disguises they were dressed up as pirates.

    ....

5. Only one of these dashes is needed. Cross out the two dashes that aren't needed.

    "I think you should — drink milk — I've drunk it — all my life."

6. Here are some statements about when you should use bullet points.
    Put a tick after the ones that are correct.

    *   At the start of different items in a vertical list, like this one. ☐

    *   To show that you are quoting someone's exact words. ☐

    *   At the end of a sentence. ☐

    *   To show that the person speaking has a mouthful of cheese. ☐

    *   To separate points in a long piece of text, to make it easier to read. ☐

Punctuation Pythons know dashes better than their own forked tongues. Tick a box to show how you measure up.

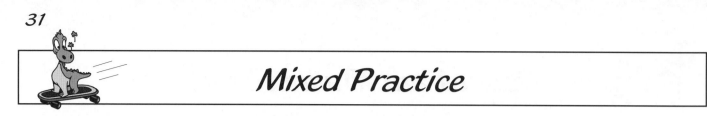

Mixed Practice

These pages will test you on lots of different punctuation marks — so stay focused.

1. Draw a line from the name of each punctuation mark, through what it looks like, to what it is used for.

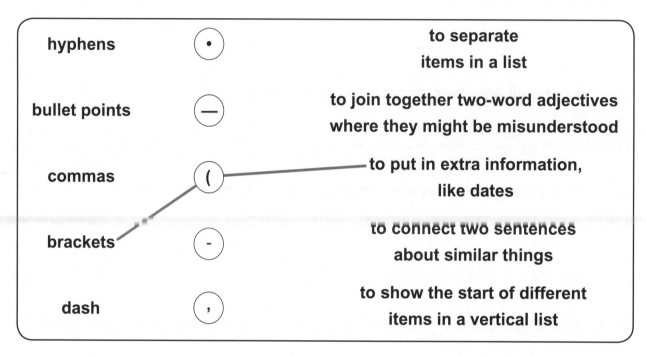

hyphens	•	to separate items in a list
bullet points	—	to join together two-word adjectives where they might be misunderstood
commas	(	to put in extra information, like dates
brackets	-	to connect two sentences about similar things
dash	,	to show the start of different items in a vertical list

2. Rewrite this sentence, adding in punctuation marks where they are needed.

    My best friend, Alan is two thirds of the way through his jigsaw.

    ....

    ....

3. These sentences all have a punctuation mark missing.
    Put the correct punctuation mark in the space provided.

    The *Alpine* (built in 1994 ... sailed into Plymouth.

    This has been a great success ... you will all be awarded a jam sandwich.

    This train stops at Halden ... Colebury and Great Bream.

    I had a part ... time job, working as a jelly taster.

Mixed Practice

4. Write something in each gap to complete the sentence

   a) The paints are in the big cupboard — ....

   .... — put them back when you're done.

   b) Christmas (...) comes
      but once a year.

   c) Alan is very tall (...).

5. This sentence is missing a punctuation mark. On the dotted line, write down what it is.

   > "The old mill, which had been shut for years was now up and running."

   The missing mark is: ....

6. One comma, one dash, one hyphen and two brackets are missing from this paragraph.
   Copy out the paragraph, putting the missing punctuation marks in the correct places.

   **It was Phyllis who had the most prize winning chickens. She won first
   prize for three breeds Sebright Sussex and Dorking and the grand prize.
   This is her last year competing she's decided to focus all her attention
   on her parrots.**

   ....

   ....

   ....

   ....

   ....

Mixed Practice

7. Put either a comma or a dash into the gaps in the sentences below.

    Don't tell me which pie to pick ... I can choose one for myself.

    However hard I try ... I can't seem to learn the penny whistle.

    If you borrow the scissors ... you must put them back on the right hanger.

    I am the strongest man in the world ... I could carry your van on my back.

    We know that you did it ... the evidence is all over your face.

8. Each column has some information that isn't correct.
    Put a line through the wrong information.

Hyphens	Dashes	Commas
are usually longer than dashes	can join two sentences together	are used to separate items in a list
are sometimes used after prefixes, such as 're'	can be used in pairs to give extra information	can be used to separate different parts of a sentence
can join two-word adjectives together	always come after another punctuation mark	can never go inside a pair of brackets

9. The recipe below is supposed to be set out in a vertical list with bullet points.
    How many bullet points does it need?

    one egg two or three pieces of bacon a frying pan some cooking oil

    This recipe needs .... bullet points.

Mixed Practice

10. All the punctuation marks you need are already in the paragraph — they are just in the wrong places. Rewrite the paragraph with the punctuation marks in the correct places.

> **Red kangaroos are odd looking-beasts which live in Australia. They have pointy snouts long, tails and big ears. The females have a, pouch. They aren't — small animals they are the biggest kangaroos in the world. They are usually quite peaceful)unless you attack them(but if one does get too close, to you here's, what to do — • drop to the ground curl up in a ball • • stay calm until it moves away**

....

....

....

....

....

....

....

....

....

....

Punctuation Pythons never fail to put the right mark in place. How much of a Punctuation Python are you?

Colons

If you use colons correctly then you'll be a cool-un. See how you get on with these questions.

1. Draw a line to match each punctuation mark to its name.

    | . | | **semi-colon** |

    | ; | | **comma** |

    | , | | **full stop** |

    | : | | **colon** |

    Colons can only join two sentences if the second sentence explains the first, or tells you more about it.

2. Put colons in the correct places so that these sentences make sense.

    We can't come [ ] to the party [ ] we are going on holiday.

    We are still hungry [ ] the shop [ ] has run out [ ] of sandwiches.

    You will need [ ] to bring camping stuff [ ] a tent, hiking shoes [ ] and a torch.

    He doesn't [ ] like camping [ ] he is worried about spiders.

    To make the mixture, you need three ingredients [ ] eggs, milk [ ] and sugar.

    I have [ ] lost my shoes [ ] they went missing [ ] from my room.

3. Rewrite these sentences, adding in colons in the correct places.

    The birds are beautiful their feathers shine.

    ....

    Harry had won the prize a trip to the moon.

    ....

Colons

4. Tick the sentences which are correct.

We found your house easily: your instructions were great. ☐

There is a flying saucer outside: it's half past nine. ☐

The sink was empty: all the water had drained out. ☐

School is cancelled: the teachers are on strike. ☐

They bought lots of fish: they did not buy any chips. ☐

5. The box below contains three sentences that are jumbled up. Draw a line from the beginning of each sentence to the end, going through the colon in the right place.

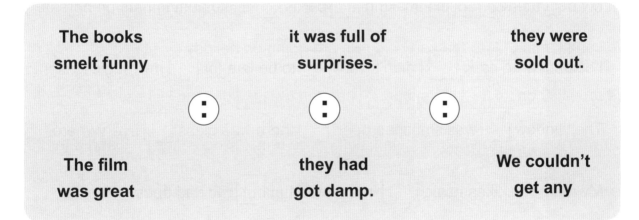

6. Use the words in the box to complete the sentence below.

| their | made | heads | are | jelly | of |

You only need to know one thing: ....

....

Semi-Colons

These punctuation marks just keep coming. But wait... this is the last one... hooray!

1. Tick or cross to show whether you can replace the underlined **conjunction** with a semi-colon.

    They packed their superhero costumes <u>and</u> went out.

    He's coming tonight <u>so</u> you should wear something nice.

    I really want to go <u>but</u> I can't make it.

    Jane was excited <u>when</u> she realised she'd won.

    Only use semi-colons to join together two <u>complete</u> sentences.

2. Put semi-colons in the correct boxes so that these sentences make sense.

    My best friend ☐ likes making ☐ cards ☐ I like putting hats on horses.

    I disappeared early ☐ I didn't want ☐ to be late for ☐ my magic lesson.

    The window ☐ was smashed open ☐ there was glass ☐ everywhere.

    My mum ☐ likes to sing ☐ in the morning ☐ my dad doesn't like it.

    The fireman went through ☐ the wreckage ☐ he was looking ☐ for clues.

3. Write in the semi-colons where they are needed.

    If you use semi-colons to separate the items in a list, you <u>do</u> need to have one before the 'and'.

    They're out to get you they know you stole it.

    It was very successful it made a lot of money.

    Cats should not be fed cornflakes they need cat food.

    We put the old, smelly suitcase the table, which had once cost thousands if not tens of thousands and the wooden donkey on the bonfire.

Semi-Colons

4. **Semi-colons** are needed in these lists. Add **semi-colons** in the appropriate places.

They saw a juggler, who was their favourite a clown, who threw custard pies and a tiger who jumped through tyres.

You need to bring spare clothes, in case you get wet a towel, to dry yourself off and some old trainers.

She always made sure that she had her pencil her rubber, because she always changed her mind her scissors and her sharpener.

We wanted to go to the zoo, to see the lions the museum to look at fossils and the bowling alley, so we couldn't decide.

5. Tick or cross to show whether all the semi-colons have been used correctly.

He bought a box of chocolates; and a hand-made card. ☐

I want to make sure she is okay; I think I still have her mobile number. ☐

They teach you about baking; I've always wanted to learn more about it. ☐

6. Write two of your own sentences which use a semi-colon.
Include the phrases 'My friend likes' and 'I like' in each one.

1. ....

2. ....

Sssemi-colons are about as slippery as a snake, or a Punctuation Python. How snake-like were you?

Mixed Practice

Time to put your colon and semi-colon skills to the test — here's a lovely mix of questions...

1. Write **semi-colons** in the sentences that are missing them. Some of the sentences don't need any — if they don't, just put a tick in the box.

    My cousin Ronny bought some raisins I found a bag of flour.

    She made the cake for everyone she hoped they'd like it.

    He liked eating Brussels sprout lasagne, while she liked starfish strudel.

    In the fruit bowl there were apples, bananas, grapes and oranges.

    The giraffes got angry the racoons were frightened.

2. The punctuation in some of these sentences is wrong. Rewrite those sentences with the correct punctuation. If the sentence is correct, just put a tick on the dotted line.

    He runs a shop: she flies a hot air balloon.

    ....

    Britain faces a serious problem: ninja foxes.

    ....

    We need three things: frogs, worms and gingerbread.

    ....

    She was smartly dressed: I was wearing my bow tie.

    ....

Mixed Practice

3. Copy out this passage, adding in colons and semi-colons in the correct places. There are **four** missing punctuation marks in total. Don't change any existing punctuation.

Jerry couldn't believe his eyes there were hundreds of kittens in waistcoats on the bus with him. There had to be a sensible explanation either he was dreaming, going mad or it was a practical joke.

Just then one of the kittens said, "My one's made of velvet George's is silk!"

Jerry screamed and suddenly found himself on his sofa. He must've been dreaming he knew he shouldn't have eaten cheese before bedtime.

....

....

....

....

....

....

....

....

....

....

Punctuation Pythons can spot a punctuation mark in long grass from up to a mile away. How about you?

Section 5 — Mixed Practice

Mixed Practice

So, you think you know all there is to know about punctuation? Let's see...

1. These sentences are missing punctuation marks. Draw a line to match each sentence to the missing punctuation mark.

   You might have to use som punctuation marks for mor than one sentence.

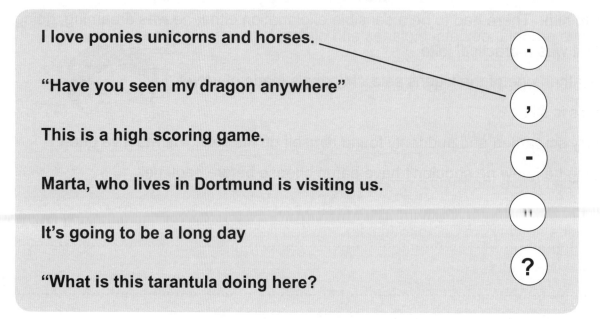

I love ponies unicorns and horses.

"Have you seen my dragon anywhere"

This is a high scoring game.

Marta, who lives in Dortmund is visiting us.

It's going to be a long day

"What is this tarantula doing here?

(.) (,) (-) (") (?)

2. Each of these sentences is missing either a colon, a semi-colon or a dash. Put the correct punctuation mark in each box to make the sentences correct.

   "Alex — whose birthday is today ☐ is throwing a party."

   I have a pet pterodactyl ☐ Jesper has a pet griffin.

   I ate a good lunch ☐ a banana, two cakes and a flask of grasshopper soup.

3. This sentence is missing some words. Add some words of your own so that the sentence makes sense and is punctuated correctly.

   I'm going to go bowling, ..., ... and .... ;

   Duncan — .... — is going ....

Mixed Practice

4. Read these sentences. Put a tick in the box next to the sentences which are correct. Underline the mistakes in the sentences that are incorrect.

a. "He's not going to enjoy it — he'll hate it." ☐

b. I love aeroplanes: jets, biplanes and gliders. ☐

c. "Don't panic, but there's a snake on your head?" ☐

d. Its Thursday evening. ☐

e. "I didn't leave the rhino's cage unlocked.' ☐

f. Their's no way I'm going to Alaska dressed like this. ☐

5. Draw lines to match these sentences to the correct term.

Ben asked if he could go outside.	reported speech
Why is your dad hiding behind the fence?	question
Get down before you hurt yourself!	direct speech
"Looks like rain on Venus today."	command

6. Rewrite these sentences with the correct punctuation.

"I've had enough: Im going home,

....

'divesh bought three things; chips; cheese, and gravy?"

....

Mixed Practice

7. Rewrite this sentence using **direct speech** and a **contraction**.

    Stefan said that he would not like to play the tuba.

    ....

8. This paragraph is missing some punctuation marks. Fix the paragraph by putting
    punctuation marks in the correct boxes.

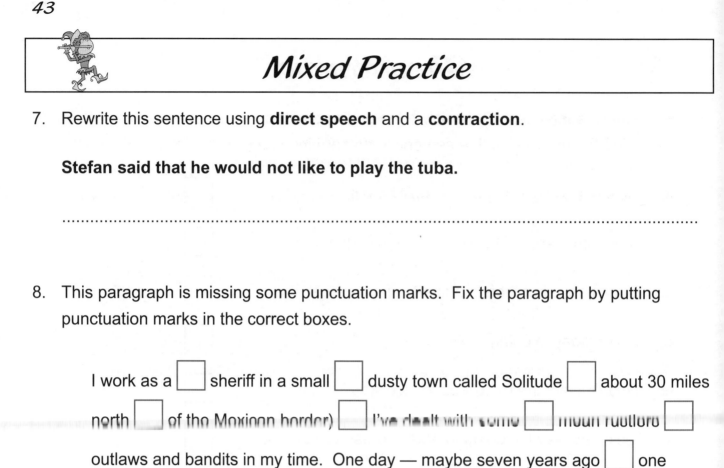

    I work as a ☐ sheriff in a small ☐ dusty town called Solitude ☐ about 30 miles
    north ☐ of the Mexican border) ☐ I've dealt with some ☐ mean rustlers ☐
    outlaws and bandits in my time. One day — maybe seven years ago ☐ one
    tough ☐ looking lawbreaker ☐ challenged me to a fight ☐ a pillow fight.

9. There are **six** mistakes in this paragraph. Circle the **six** punctuation mistakes,
    then rewrite the paragraph and correct the mistakes.

    > **The funquabs that live on jupiter are a curious mixture of lions and chickens,**
    > **The funquab has two legs two wings, a bushy mane and a tail. It's other**
    > **features are just as interesting; a beak, whiskers and razor sharp claws.**

    ....

    ....

    ....

    ....

*Only a Punctuation Python would get every question
right. Are you a Punctuation Python?*

Proofreading

Proofreading is about reading something very carefully to see if you want to make any changes or improvements, but also to spot any mistakes. For these passages you're just looking for the punctuation errors — there are <u>fifteen</u> in each.

1. Draw a circle round the errors. Then rewrite the passage, correcting the mistakes.

> "right, thats it! Everybody out on strike?" shouted Rex the sheep
>
> "This grass is useless and I want something done about it! he bleated" from the top of a rust stained wheelbarrow
>
> rex his real name was Burt Jenkin's) stood proudly in front of the crowd. The other sheep arranged themselves in height order; tallest at the back and shortest at the front. There was a lot of excitement, because Rex was an ex politician.
>
> "I have several complaints about our grass; it's not sweet, long green or juicy enough. I demand to know why!"

....

....

....

....

....

....

....

....

....

Proofreading

2. There are **15** punctuation errors in this passage. Circle each error, and then rewrite the passage underneath. If you run out of space, use an extra piece of paper to write on.

Bryony flew down the stairs, almost tripping over Nathans' micro-scooter.

"Why does he always leave that thing there!" screamed Bryony: pouring milk on her toast and putting marmalade in her tea. This was an important day for Bryony: It was the last day of her SATs, and Mrs Whinge had organised a last minute class party.

Did you have exams when you were at school, Mum" asked Bryony

"In my day," replied Mum (who was known for her sarcasm, "it was all dinosaur catching and cave painting"

"I think wed better be going now, don't you, young lady? Mum wiped the marmalade from her daughters chin and picked up her car keys. bryony still had marmalade in her hair, but she didnt care because today was the end of her SATs.

....

....

....

....

....

....

....

....

Punctuation Pythons would gobble up these questions for breakfast. How have you got on with them?

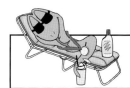

Glossary

COMMON PUNCTUATION MARKS

Apostrophes — show **missing letters** and **belonging**. `,`

Brackets — **separate extra information** in a sentence. `( )`

Bullet points — **separate** different points in a **list**. `•`

Capital letters — used for **proper nouns** and for **starting** sentences. `A`

Colons — **Introduce some lists** and **join sentences**. `:`

Commas — **separate** items in a **list**, separate **extra information** in a sentence and **join clauses**. `,`

Dashes — **separate extra information** in a sentence. `—`

Exclamation marks — show **strong feeling** or **commands**. `!`

Full stops — show where **sentences end**. `.`

Hyphens — **link words** or parts of words to make the meaning clear. `-`

Inverted commas — show **direct speech**. `" "`

Question marks — used at the **end** of **questions**. `?`

Semi-colons — **separate lists** of **longer things** and **join sentences**. `;`

USEFUL WORDS

Command — A **sentence** that **tells** somebody to **do something**.

Direct speech — The **actual words** that are **said** by someone.

Proper noun — A **noun** that is the **name** of a **specific person**, **place** or **thing**.

Question — A **sentence** that **asks something**.

Reported speech — What someone has said, but **not in their own words**.

Statement — A **sentence** that **gives information**.